Distance

BLACKBIRCH PRESS

An imprint of Thomson Gale, a part of The Thomson Corporation

Detroit • New York • San Francisco • San Diego • New Haven, Conn. • Waterville, Maine • London • Munich

Consultant: Kimi Hosoume
Associate Director of GEMS (Great Explorations in Math and Science),
Director of PEACHES (Primary Explorations for Adults, Children, and Educators in Science),
Lawrence Hall of Science,
University of California,
Berkeley, California

For The Brown Reference Group plc
Text: Chris Woodford
Project Editor: Lesley Campbell-Wright
Designer: Lynne Ross
Picture Researcher: Susy Forbes
Illustrator: Darren Awuah
Managing Editor: Bridget Giles
Children's Publisher: Anne O'Daly
Production Director: Alastair Gourlay
Editorial Director: Lindsey Lowe

For more information, contact
Blackbirch Press
27500 Drake Rd.
Farmington Hills, MI 48331-3535
Or you can visit our Internet site at http://www.gale.com

PHOTOGRAPHIC CREDITS
The Brown Reference Group plc: Edward Allwright 28, 29; **Corbis:** Ron Boardman/FLPA 16, Jim Craigmyle 27b, Stapleton Collection 6; **David Noble Photography:** 23t; **NASA:** 27t; **Photos.com:** 1, 7, 9, 10, 12, 18, 22, 23b; **Still Pictures:** Jochen Tack 14; **U.S. Defense:** 24.

Front cover: **The Brown Reference Group plc:** Edward Allwright

LIBRARY OF CONGRESS CATALOGING-IN-PUBLICATION DATA

Woodford, Chris.
Distance / by Chris Woodford.
p. cm. — (How do we measure?)
ISBN 1-4103-0364-0 (hardcover : alk. paper) — ISBN 1-4103-0520-1 (pbk. : alk. paper)
1. Distances—Measurement. I. Title II. Series: Woodford, Chris. How do we measure?

QC102.W66 2005
530.8—dc22

2004017613

Printed and bound in Thailand
10 9 8 7 6 5 4 3 2 1

Contents

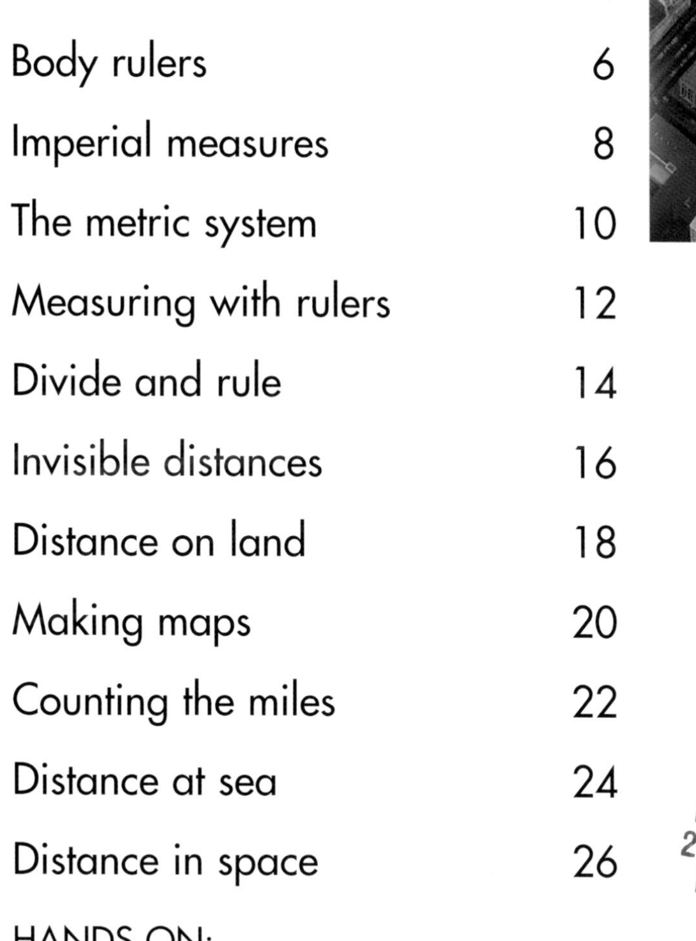

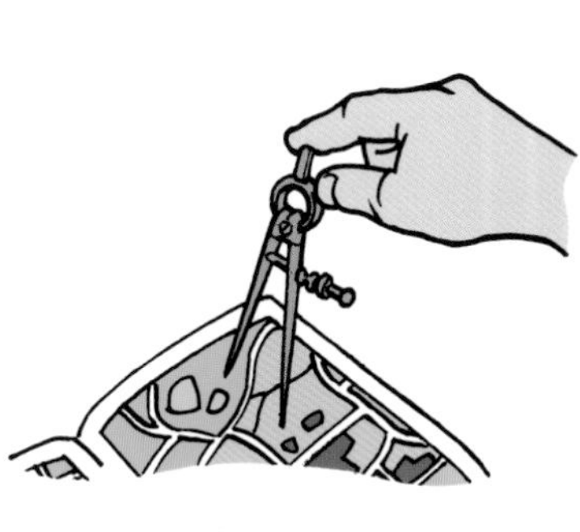

What is distance?

Have you ever gazed up at the Moon and wondered how far away it is? Or looked at a map of your town and thought about how someone drew it? Perhaps you might have wondered how long a whale is. Questions like that involve distance.

Distance and length are the sam

This line is 1 inch long.

1 foot = 12 inches

1 yard = 3 feet = 36 inches

1 mile = 1,760 yards = 5,280 feet

A blue whale measures 100 feet long.

Why measure distance?

There are lots of reasons why we need to measure distance. You might want to know if a pair of jeans will be long enough to fit your legs or big enough around the waist. A family driving to another town needs to know how far away it is so they can figure out how much gas to put in the tank and when they will arrive.

The Empire State Building in New York City is 1,250 feet high.

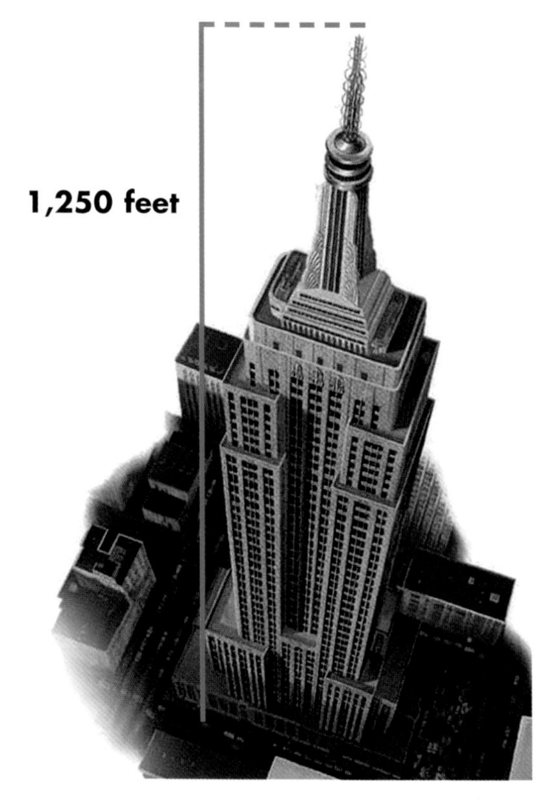

Distance is a measurement of how long, tall, or far away something is. One kind of distance is length. Length is the distance from one end of an object to the other. Height is another kind of distance. It is a measure of how tall something is. The height of a building is the distance from the ground to the very top.

People can measure distance along a straight line using all kinds of tools. These tools include rulers made of wood, plastic, or metal; tapes, which bend easily; and laser beams (strong rays of light). They help people measure distances on land, at sea, and even in space.

Body rulers

In ancient times, people used parts of their body to measure distance. About 5,000 years ago, the ancient Egyptians invented a measurement called the cubit. A cubit was the distance from the tip of a person's middle finger to the elbow.

The Egyptians did not go around measuring things with their arms, though. They used sticks cut to the length of a cubit.

The ancient Greeks lived about 2,000 years ago. They measured distance with the width of their fingers. Sixteen fingers was roughly equal to the length of a person's foot. This is how the measurement the foot got its name.

In around 800 A.D. Frankish king and emperor Charlemagne (742–812) decided to make the length of his foot a standard measurement.

How many cubits?

Imagine you and your family are ancient Egyptians. Get an adult to stretch out his or her arm from the middle finger to the elbow. That measurement is a cubit. Now try measuring some things around your home in cubits. You could try measuring your bed, your sofa, or the length of a table.

The ancient Romans lived shortly after the Greeks. Instead of using fingers, like the Greeks, the Romans used the width of their thumbs. They called this measurement an uncia. The modern word *inch* comes from that same word. The Romans found that a person's foot was usually about 12 inches long. That is why there are still 12 inches in a foot.

A: 1 cubit

B: 16 finger widths = about 1 foot

C: 1 uncia = about 1 inch

D: 1 foot = about 12 inches

Imperial measures

Through the ages, people have measured distances in different ways. Many hundreds of years ago, some people measured an inch by placing three ears of barley side by side. The ancient Romans measured an inch using the width of their thumbs.

Different ways of measuring made it hard to buy and sell things. Suppose someone wanted to buy some cloth. If different traders used different measures, no one could tell how much cloth they were getting for their money. Measuring distance was very confusing.

But hundreds of years ago in Europe, during a time called the Middle Ages, most people started to use the same measurements—the inch, foot, yard, and mile. This system is usually called the imperial system. It got that name because emperors and rulers tried to make people use it. People in many countries still use the imperial system.

1 inch

In the Middle Ages some people used to measure an inch by placing three ears of barley side by side.

How long and how far?

Here are some distances measured using the imperial system:

Height of a typical person
= *5 feet 9 inches*

Length of a family car
= *18 feet*

Length of a football field
= *120 yards*

Distance from New York City to Los Angeles
= *2,500 miles*

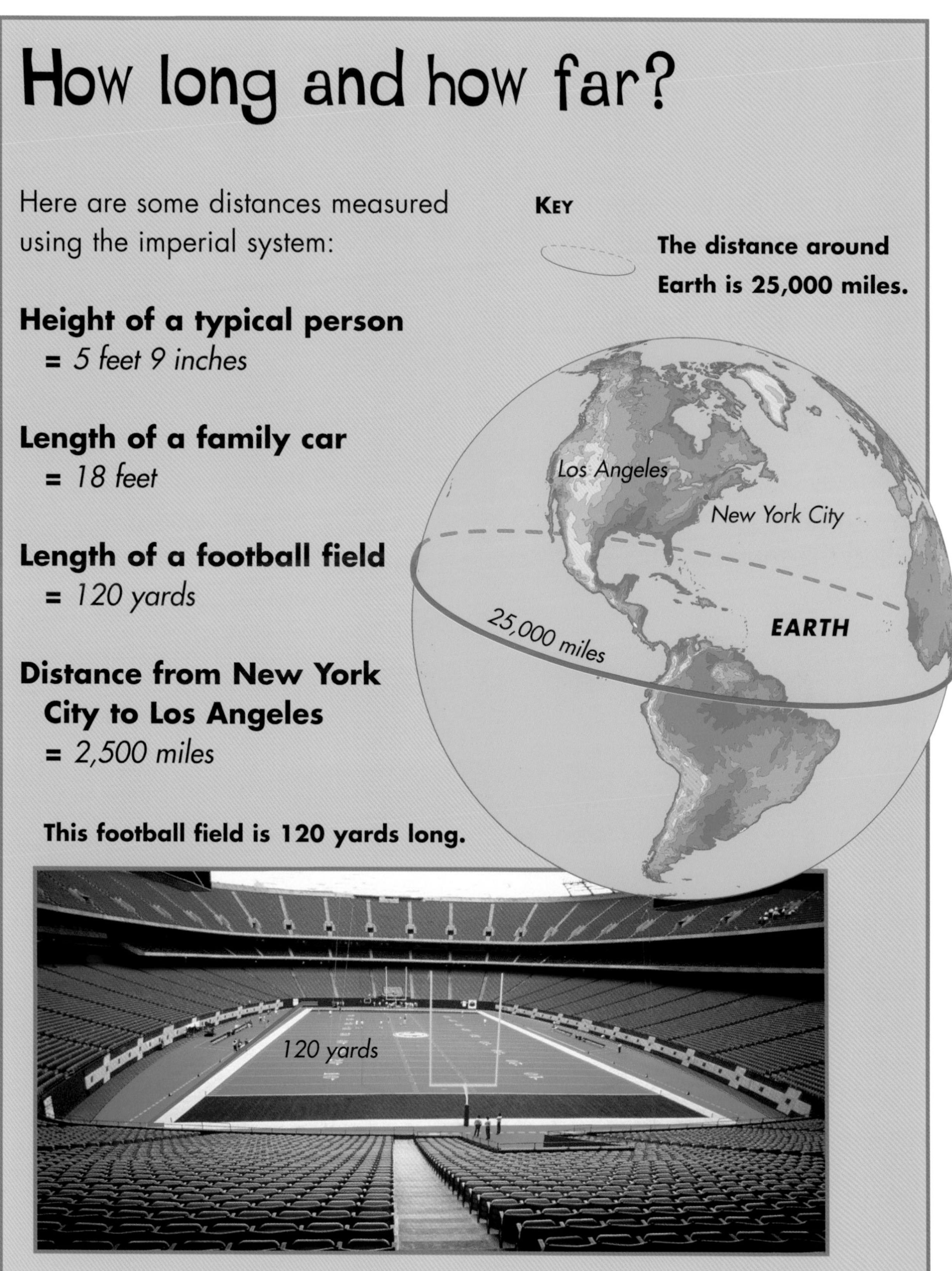

This football field is 120 yards long.

The metric system

Many people found the imperial system hard to remember. During the 18th century, the French came up with a simpler way to measure distances. Their system, called the metric system, was based on a new measurement called the meter.

A metric signpost uses kilometers (km).

Think metric

This red line is 1 centimeter long.

1 centimeter = 10 millimeters
100 centimeters = 1 meter
1,000 meters = 1 kilometer

Length of a man's finger
= 7.5 centimeters

Length around a race track
= 400 meters

Average depth of the ocean
= 3.7 kilometers

An adult flea is 3 millimeters long.

An elephant is 3 meters high.

Measuring the meter

The French were unsure how to define an exact meter. In 1799 someone had the idea of measuring the huge distance from the equator to the North Pole and then dividing it by 10 million. That distance was then called 1 meter.

In 1983 scientists decided it would be more accurate to define a meter using the speed of light. Light always travels at the same speed. One meter became the distance that light travels in one second divided by 300,000,000.

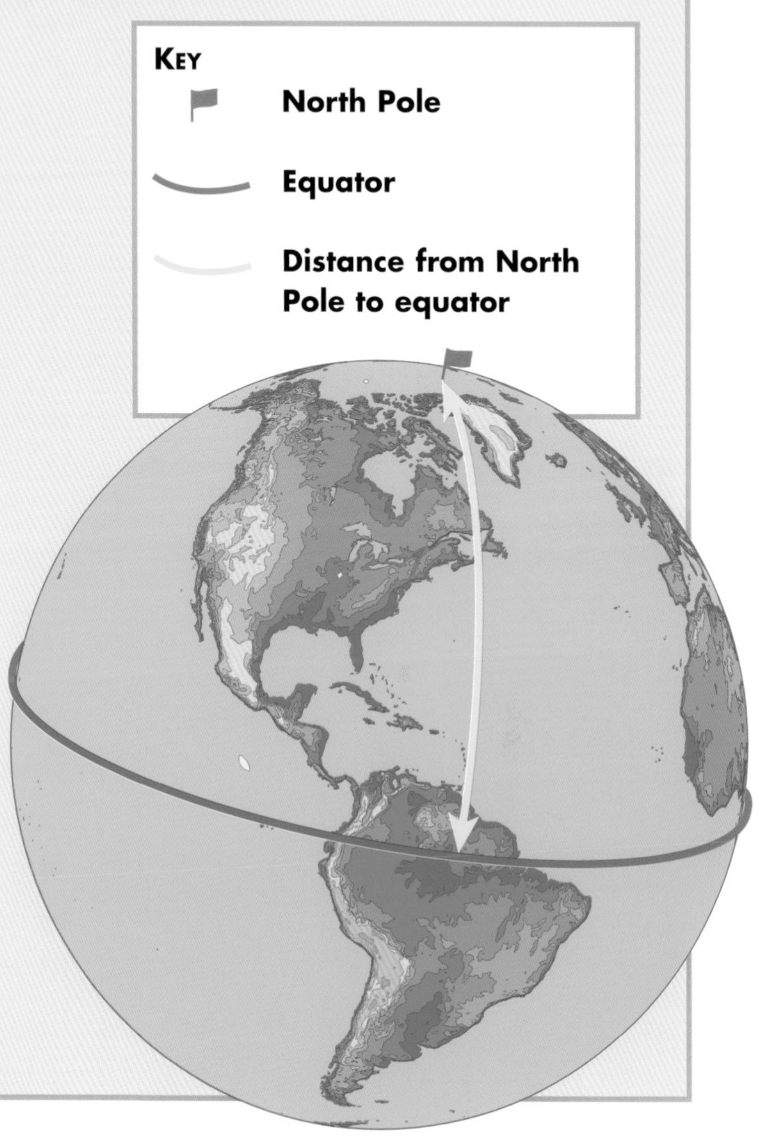

One meter is 39 inches long, which is a little longer than a yard (3 feet, or 36 inches).

The metric system is used in many countries. It is also called the International System, or SI system.

The metric system is easier to remember than the imperial system—there are 10 millimeters (mm) in a centimeter (cm), 100 centimeters in a meter (m), and 1,000 meters in a kilometer (km).

Measuring with rulers

Everyone needs to measure things in exactly the same way. They do this by using a standard measuring tool, such as a ruler. A ruler is a piece of wood, plastic, or metal marked with exact measurements.

Rulers are usually about 1 foot (30 centimeters) or 1 yard (90 centimeters) long. One-yard rulers are called yardsticks. Another kind of ruler—a meterstick—is 1 meter (39 inches) long.

Rulers can be used to measure distances that are either bigger or smaller than the ruler itself. Most rulers are marked with smaller units such as inches, centimeters, or millimeters. A person can measure larger things by moving the ruler along and counting how many times it fits into a distance.

Longer distances are easier to measure with a tape. A tape measure is like a long ruler made of soft plastic or cloth. A tape can measure around curved surfaces, such as your waist.

Tape measures are made of soft materials that can measure curves.

Imperial to metric and back again

People often have to change imperial measurements into metric measurements, or metric measurements into imperial measurements.

This girl is 4 foot 6 inches, or 137 centimeters, tall (137 centimeters is the same as 1 meter and 37 centimeters).

Imperial to metric

1 inch is the same as 2.5 centimeters, or 25 millimeters
1 foot is the same as 30 centimeters
1 yard is the same as 90 centimeters
1 mile is the same as 1,600 meters, or 1.6 kilometers

Metric to imperial

1 centimeter is the same as 0.4 inches
1 meter is the same as 3 feet 3 inches, or 39 inches
1 kilometer is the same as 0.6 miles

Divide and rule

Sometimes people need to measure small distances on a map, the thickness of a piece of wire, or the length of a small animal. The best way to measure accurately such things is with dividers, calipers, or gauges.

Dividers are like the compasses people use to draw circles. To measure the distance between two points on a map, the two legs of the dividers are opened and one leg is put on each point. Then the distance between the divider legs is measured against the map scale.

The diameter (width) of an apple may be measured by placing it in a caliper. When the apple is removed, a ruler may be used to measure the distance between the caliper legs.

A gauge has slots of different sizes cut into it. The size of a piece of wire can be measured simply by matching it up with the slot of the same size. Then the measurement can be read on the gauge.

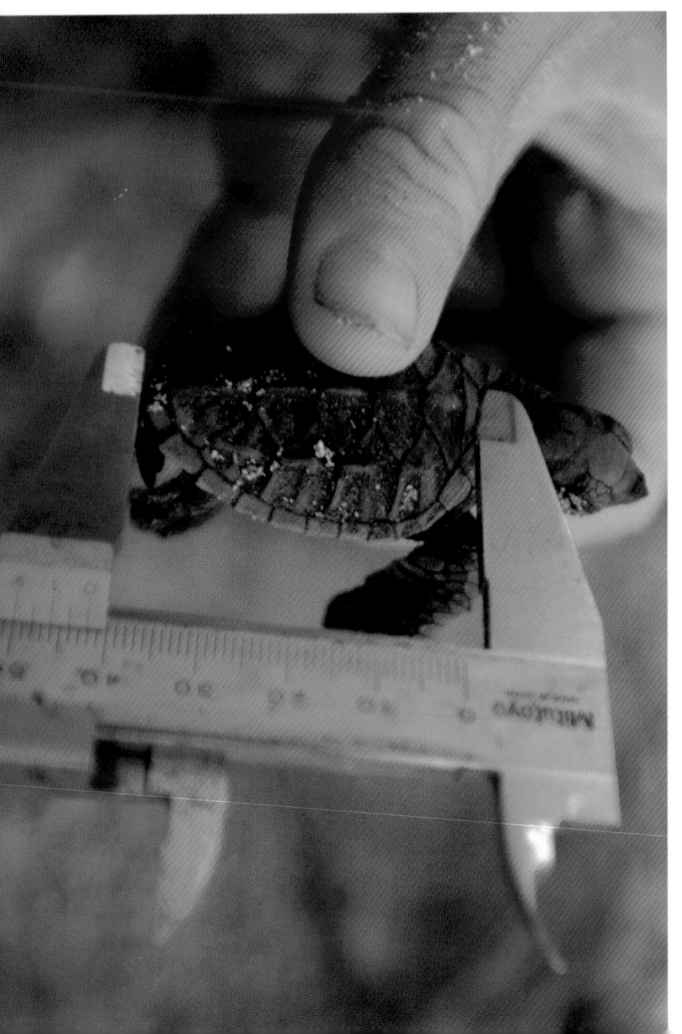

A caliper is used to measure the length of a turtle's shell.

Micrometer

A micrometer is a type of caliper with a built-in measuring scale. A micrometer is shaped like the letter C. It very accurately measures the width of an object placed between its jaws.

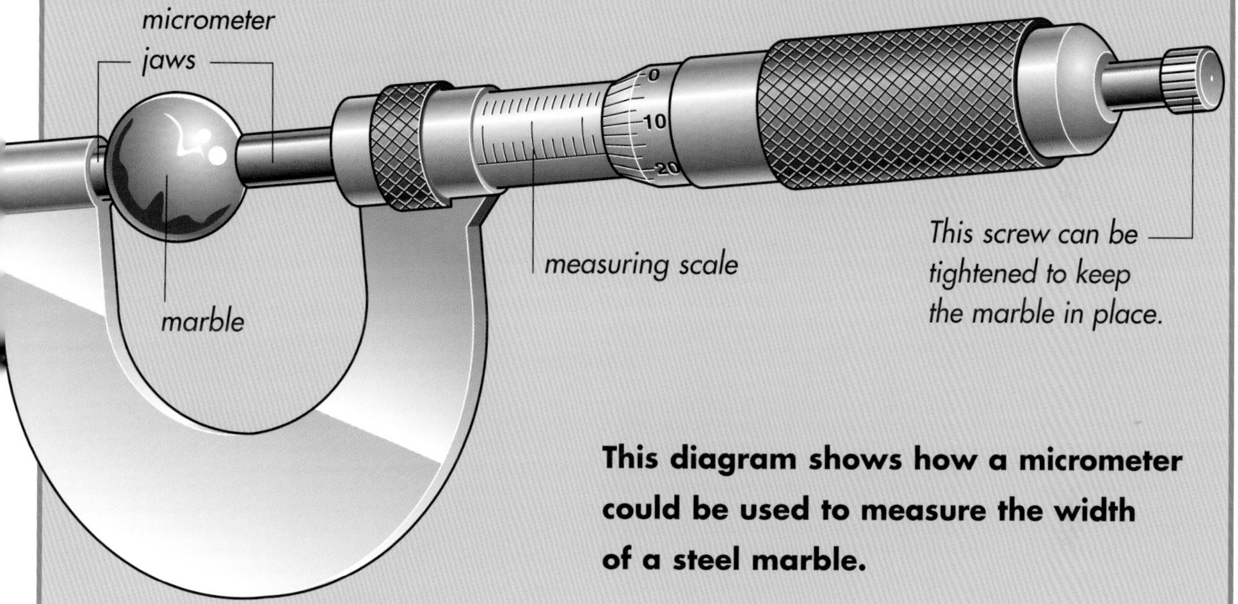

micrometer jaws

marble

measuring scale

This screw can be tightened to keep the marble in place.

0 10 20

This diagram shows how a micrometer could be used to measure the width of a steel marble.

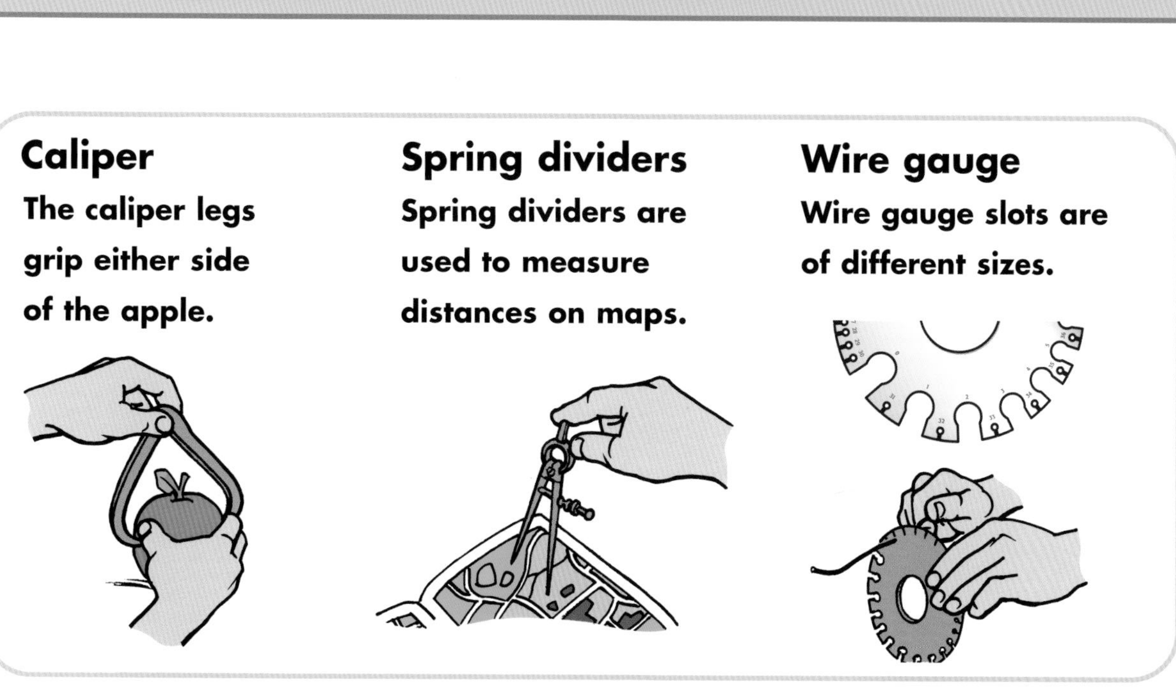

Caliper

The caliper legs grip either side of the apple.

Spring dividers

Spring dividers are used to measure distances on maps.

Wire gauge

Wire gauge slots are of different sizes.

Invisible distances

It is possible for people to measure distances that are too small to see. The length of something like a tiny bug can be measured with a simple microscope, for example. A microscope is a special tool with lenses that make tiny objects appear much larger. Lenses are slices of polished and curved glass. Some microscopes have a ruler built into the eyepiece. The size of an object can be seen by lining it up with this ruler. Both the ruler and the object are magnified (made to look larger)

This tiny bug has been magnified many times to make it visible.

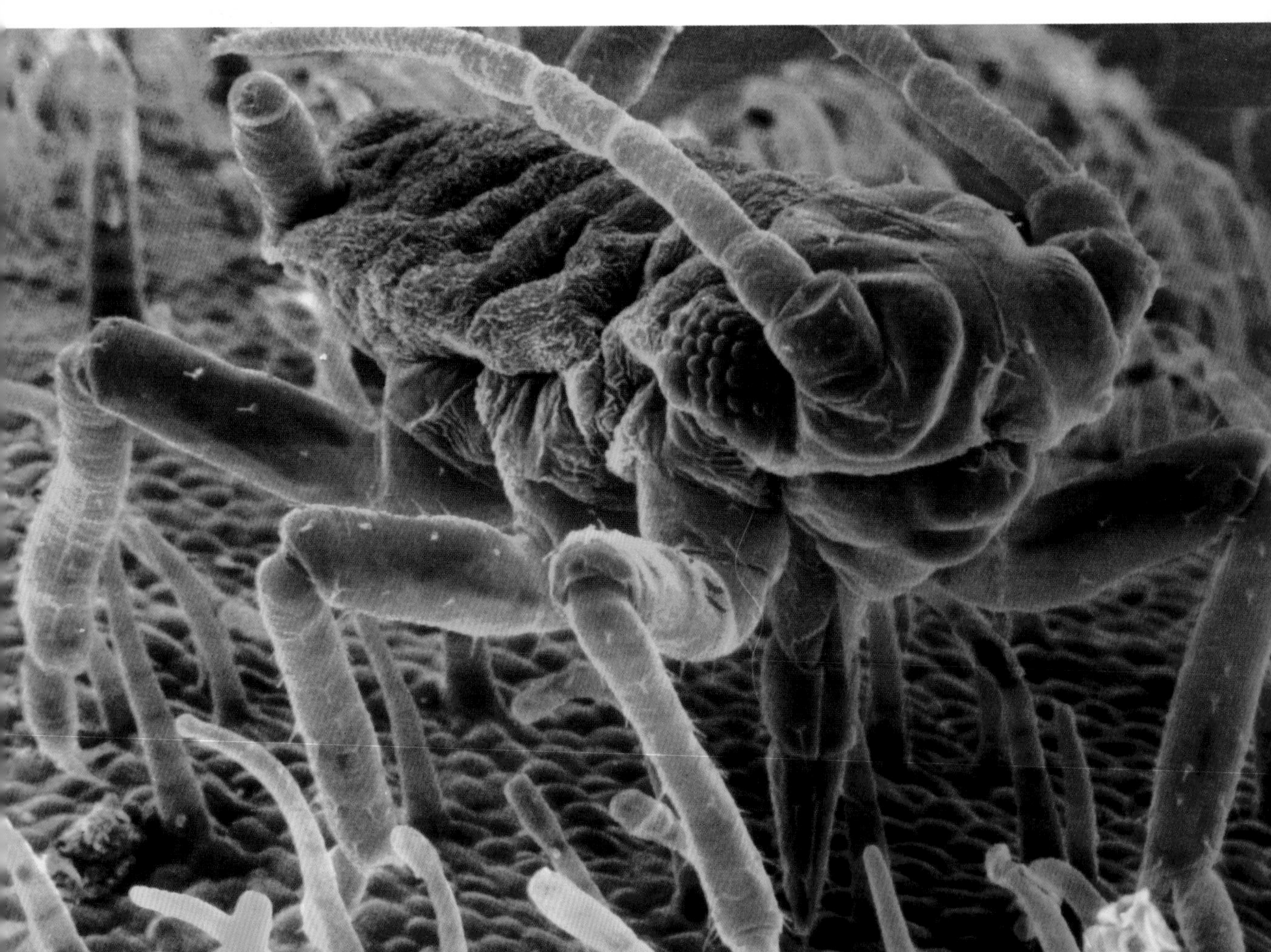

Measuring nanotechnology

Nanotechnology is one of the most exciting areas of science. It involves building new materials, medicines, and other things from incredibly tiny parts. Each part is just a few nanometers across.

A nanometer is one-billionth of a meter. It is hard to imagine a distance so small, but a tiny speck of dust may be about only 3 nanometers wide. Put another way, if a nanometer was as big as the width of a pin head, a meter would be as long as the distance between Washington, D.C., and Atlanta, Georgia, which is about 630 miles, or 1,000 kilometers!

Nanotechnology is a bit like using a super-small building set. Scientists work in this small world using extremely powerful microscopes. They look through the microscope to put the tiny pieces together.

atom

Two tiny nanotubes made from minute particles called atoms.

by the microscope. Some microscope lenses magnify about 10 times normal size, while others magnify things about 1,500 times.

Other microscopes have a micrometer built into them. By looking at the micrometer scale, an object's size can be determined.

Distance on land

Suppose a person wanted to plan the route of a freeway. Rulers and microscopes are not much help. Instead, people need tools for measuring long distances. In the past, people measured distances using clumsy metal chains. These chains were like huge folding rulers.

Miles and miles of road stretch out behind a truck. Such enormous distances cannot be measured simply by using rulers.

Each chain had 100 metal links. Each link was 8 inches (20 centimeters) long, so the whole chain stretched to about 66 feet (20 meters). People measured long distances by laying chains end to end. It took 80 chains to make 1 mile (1.6 kilometers).

Laser rulers

Earth does not have a flat, smooth surface. Hills, rivers, mountains, and valleys make it hard to measure distances with long chains. So people now measure distances using instruments called theodolites. A theodolite is an instrument that can measure angles or distances very accurately.

A theodolite sits atop a tripod. A tripod is a stand with three legs. It keeps the theodolite steady. Another tripod, with a mirror on top, is placed at the point to be measured. A person presses a button. The theodolite fires a laser beam to the mirror. The mirror bounces the beam back. A computer in the theodolite figures out how far away the mirror is and shows the result on a screen.

The theodolite fires a laser beam (red line) to the mirror on the tripod. The mirror bounces the beam back (blue line).

Theodolite fires laser beams.

laser beams

Making maps

Tools such as chains and theodolites are useful for planning highways and buildings. They are also very important for drawing maps. A map is a picture of a place seen from above. For a map to be useful, it must show where

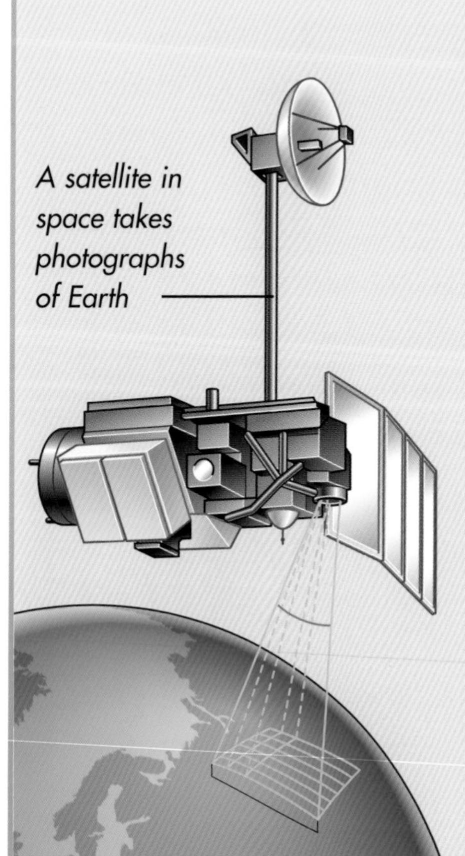

A satellite in space takes photographs of Earth

Old and new maps

The first maps of the United States were made by people who never even went there. They were drawn by mapmakers living in Europe in the 1500s. These mapmakers had very little information. All they had were the letters and stories sent back by explorers. Mapmaking is now very different. Mapmakers take photographs of towns and cities from airplanes or satellites. A satellite is an object that orbits, or moves around, Earth hundreds of miles above the ground in space. People make maps from these photographs by tracing on top of them.

A view of part of a town from above shows where all the buildings, roads, and railroads are.

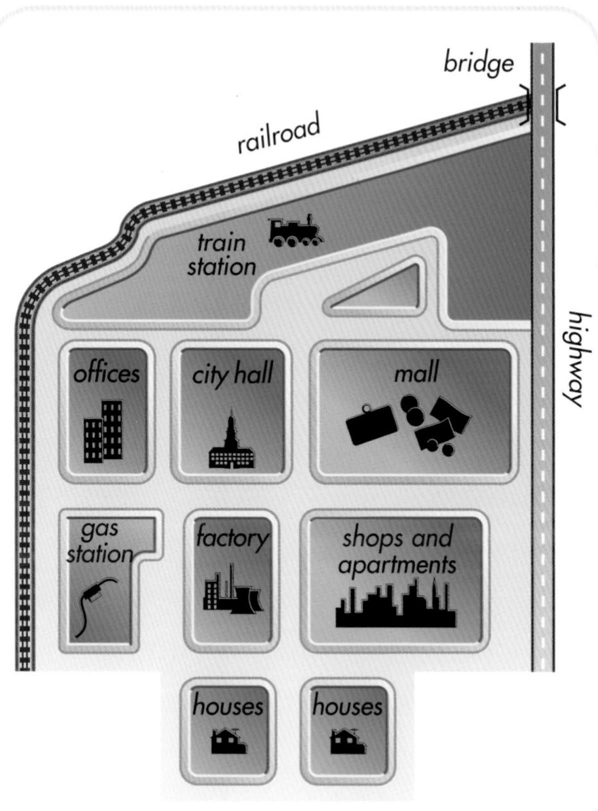

This is a simple map of the same part of town. Which road is Main Street?

things are and how far away one thing is from another. Measuring distances is very important for making maps. Maps usually have a scale drawn on them. A scale is like a picture of a ruler. The scale shows how big the things on the map really are. A common scale is for 1 inch (2.5 centimeters) to equal 10 miles (16 kilometers). So a street that is 1 inch (2.5 centimeters) long on the map is 10 miles (16 kilometers) long in real life.

Counting the miles

When people are traveling long distances, they need to know how far they have gone. Cars and motorcycles have a counter on the dashboard that measures the distance traveled. That counter is called an odometer. It works by counting how many times the car's wheels turn around.

For example, if a car wheel is 60 inches (150 centimeters) around the outside edge (its circumference), each time the wheel turns around once, the car has traveled a distance of 60 inches (150 cm). An odometer counts how many times the wheels turn. Since it knows the wheels' size, the

Marvelous miles

Some people have traveled amazing distances to break world records. The farthest distance anyone has pushed themselves in a wheelchair is about 112 miles (180 km). The world record distance traveled on a skateboard is 3,000 miles (4,800 km). It took 26 days to go this far. The longest ever taxi ride was 21,691 miles (34,706 km). This record-breaking attempt happened in 1994 and cost $63,500.

In 2003 four skateboarders set a world record when they rode their skateboards from Oregon to Virginia to raise money for charity.

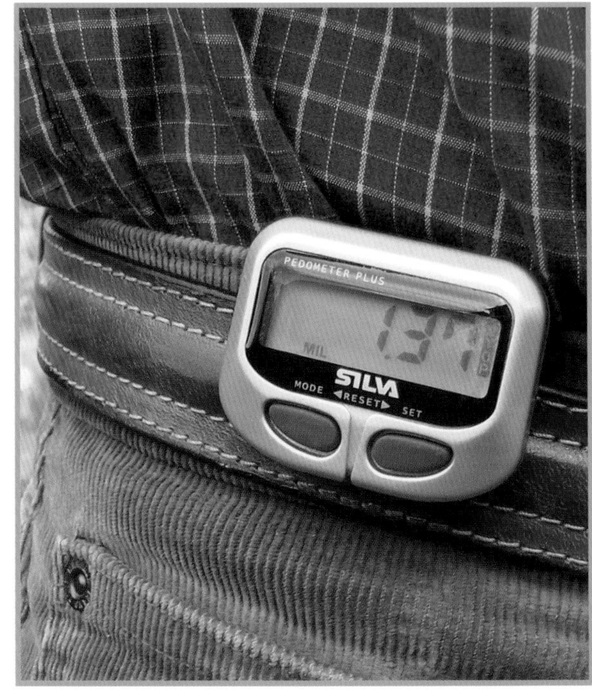

A pedometer is usually worn on the hip. It counts the number of steps a person walks. When you enter your stride length, the pedometer calculates the distance walked.

odometer can also figure out how far the car has traveled.

Walkers can use a device called a pedometer to determine how far they have walked. The pedometer is placed on their belt or sits in their pocket. As they walk, their body jiggles.

The pedometer uses this jiggling motion to figure out how far the walker has gone.

An odometer measures the distance a car travels by counting the number of times its wheels go around.

The distance around the outside edge is the wheel's circumference.

Distance at sea

Far from land, it can be difficult for ships to figure out where they are. Navigation involves measuring a position on land or at sea. Rough seas and bad weather can make it hard for ships to navigate.

In ancient times, people navigated by looking at the Sun and the stars. This method can be surprisingly accurate. A device called a sextant lets people measure how high the Sun is in the sky.

This sailor is using a sextant to measure how high the Sun is in the sky. From such measurements, she can figure out exactly where the ship is.

Using satellites

It is now much harder to get lost at sea than it was in ancient times. Now there are signals from satellites to help ships navigate. This technology is called GPS or Global Positioning System. A GPS receiver in a ship picks up signals from four different satellites. In a few seconds, the receiver can figure out a ship's position to within 50 feet (15 meters). Airplanes and missiles also use GPS.

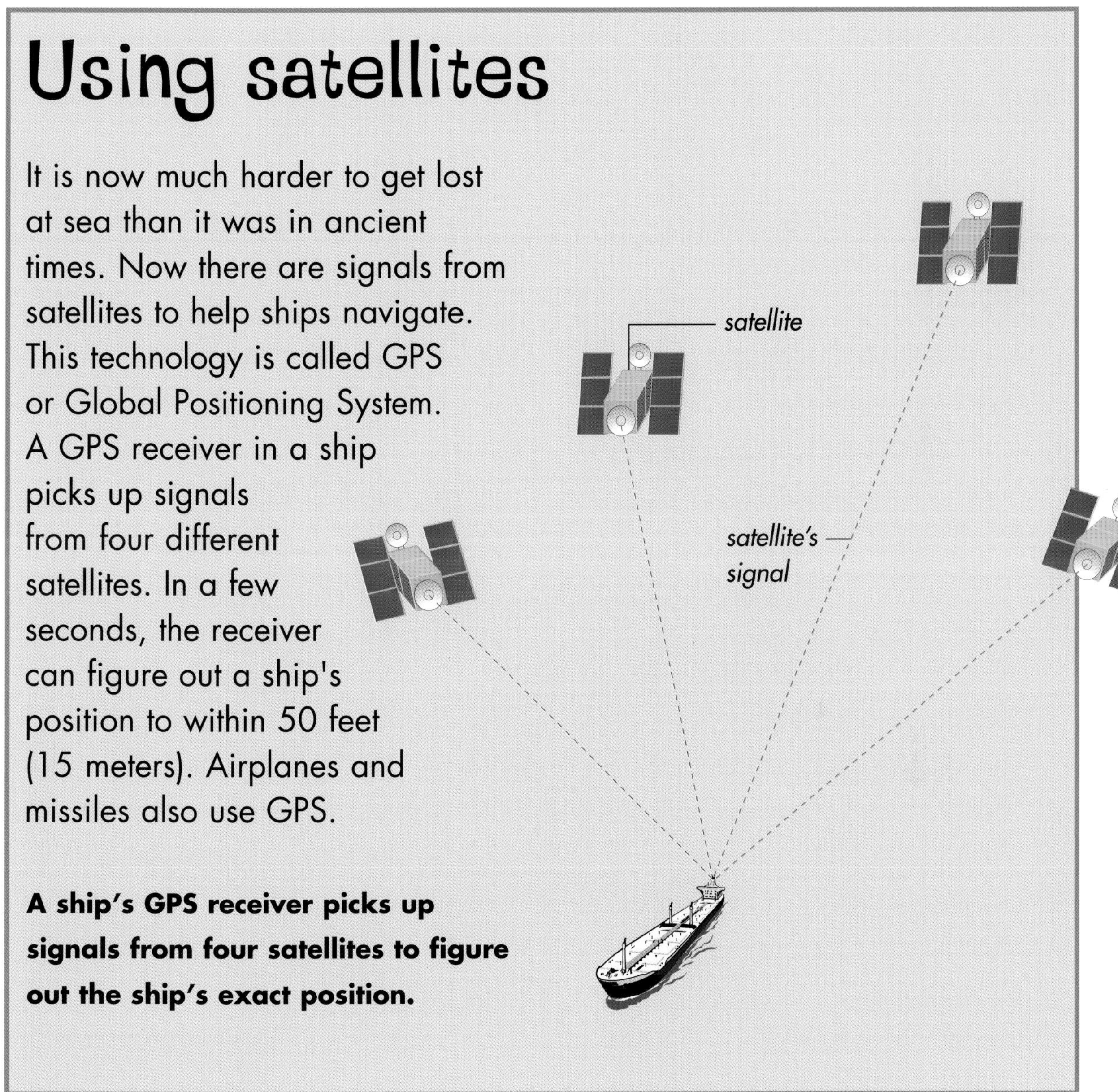

A ship's GPS receiver picks up signals from four satellites to figure out the ship's exact position.

From this measurement, a navigator can find out how far north or south the ship is.

Another way of measuring distance at sea is called dead reckoning. If a ship moves at a steady speed in a straight line, sailors can figure out how far the ship has sailed because they know how long it takes to sail one mile at a certain speed. Modern ships now navigate using signals from satellites in space.

Distance in space

Space is an enormous place. Most of the things people use to measure on Earth cannot be used to measure the immense distances between the stars and planets. Most people find it impossible to imagine what distances in space are really like.

One of the closest things to Earth is the Sun, which is 93 million miles (149 million km) away. Some objects in space are much farther away. The closest star to the Sun is 4.3 light years away. A light year is the distance that a beam of light travels in a year. It is about 6 trillion miles. It would take a jumbo jet more than one million years to fly that far!

PLANET	DISTANCE FROM SUN
1. Mercury	37 million miles (60 million km)
2. Venus	65 million miles (105 million km)
3. Earth	93 million miles (150 million km
4. Mars	130 million miles (209 million km)
5. Jupiter	484 million miles (778 million km)
6. Saturn	892 million miles (1,436 million km)
7. Uranus	1.78 billion miles (2.87 billion km)
8. Neptune	2.8 billion miles (4.5 billion km)
9. Pluto	3.66 billion miles (5.89 billion km)

Space ruler

When astronauts visited the Moon in the early 1970s (right), they placed small mirrors on its surface. Scientists on Earth fired laser beams at these mirrors. They used telescopes to time how long the laser beams took to bounce back to Earth. A telescope is an instrument that uses lenses to magnify faraway things. From this result, they measured the distance from Earth to the Moon. It is nearly 250,000 miles (400,000 km).

A telescope helps people see other planets from Earth.

How long is your street?

You will need:

- A bicycle
- A friend to help you
- An adult to walk with you
- A sharp pencil
- A piece of ribbon
- A ruler
- A piece of chalk
- A pen and piece of paper
- Scissors

1 Carefully cut a small length of ribbon using the scissors. Get an adult to help you. Tie the ribbon to the outside of the bicycle tire where you can see it.

2 Turn the bicycle wheel so the ribbon is at the bottom, on the ground. Using the chalk, make a mark on the ground next to the ribbon.

3 Slowly push the bicycle along so the wheel turns around exactly once. The ribbon should move back to the bottom again. With your chalk, make a second mark on the ground, next to the ribbon.

6 Using the ruler, measure the distance between the two chalk marks. This distance is the same as the distance around the edge of your tire, or its circumference. Write down this figure.

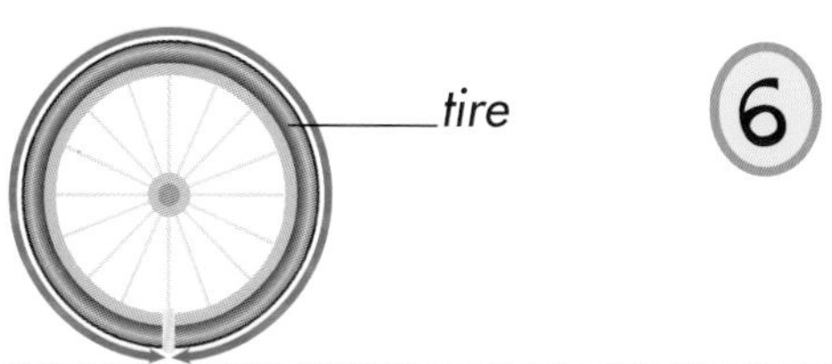

Chalk mark on street
Ribbon around tire
Distance between two chalk marks = circumference of tire

7 Take your bicycle to one end of your street. Get an adult to go with you. Turn the tire so the ribbon or tape is at the bottom.

8 Wheel the bicycle slowly along from one end of the street to the other. Count how many times the ribbon hits the pavement. That is the number of times the wheel has turned around.

9 Multiply the number of times the wheel turned by the circumference of your tire. For example, say your tire's circumference is 25 inches (64 centimeters) and the wheel has turned around 50 times. The length of your street is:

25 inches x 50 = 1,250 inches
(or 104 feet)

Or: 64 centimeters x 50 =
3,175 centimeters
(or 31.75 meters)

8

Glossary

caliper A device for measuring the distance across (width of) an object.

centimeter A small distance equal to one meter divided by 100.

cubit In ancient times, the distance from the tip of a person's middle finger to their elbow.

distance A measurement of the space between two points. Length measures distance across the ground. Height measures distance from top to bottom.

divider A tool for measuring distances on a map.

foot A distance equal to 12 inches. A foot was originally about the length of an adult's foot.

gauge A device for measuring small widths (distances across things).

inch One-twelfth of a foot. An inch was originally the width of an adult's thumb.

kilometer A metric measurement equal to 1,000 meters.

laser beam A very strong and straight beam of light.

light year The distance light travels in one year, roughly 6 trillion miles (10 trillion kilometers).

meter A metric measurement equal to about 3.3 feet.

metric A set of measurements based on the meter.

micrometer A very accurate tool for measuring small distances.

microscope A scientific instrument for magnifying very tiny things.

millimeter A tiny distance equal to 1 meter divided by 1,000.

mile A distance equal to 5,280 feet, or 1,760 yards (1.6 kilometers).

navigation A way of finding your position on Earth, at sea, or in space.

nanometer An extremely small distance, equal to one-billionth of a meter.

ruler A straight measuring tool.

satellite An uncrewed spacecraft that can measure things from space.

sextant A device used for navigating at sea. It measures the position of the Sun above the horizon. The horizon is the farthest part of Earth you can see, where the sky meets the ground.

theodolite A device that people use for measuring distances and angles.

yard A distance equal to 3 feet (90 centimeters).

Find out more

Books

Carol Vorderman, ***How Math Works.*** New York: Penguin, 1996.

Francis Thompson, ***Hands-On Math; Ready-To-Use Games and Activities For Grades 4–8***. New York: John Wiley, 2002.

Greg Tang and Harry Briggs, ***Math for All Seasons.*** New York: Scholastic, 2002.

Jerry Pallotta and Rob Bolster, ***Hershey's Milk Chocolate Weights and Measures.*** New York: Cartwheel Books/Scholastic, 2003.

Web sites

FunBrain.com Kids Center
Math and measurement games
www.funbrain.com/measure/index.html

Maps and measurements
Learn how to measure with maps
academic.brooklyn.cuny.edu/geology/leveson/core/linksa/maptop.html

Math-Kitecture
Draft a classroom plan using your measuring skills
www.math-kitecture.com

Science Made Simple
Metric conversions for length measurement
www.sciencemadesimple.net/EASYlength.html

Index